The Wayland Book of
Common
British Trees
A Photographic Guide

Theresa Greenaway

Photographs by Archie Miles

Wayland

An imprint of Hodder Children's Books

The Wayland Book of
Common British Trees
A Photographic Guide

Cover photograph: An old hornbeam (*Carpinus betulus*).
Title page: A common oak (*Quercus robur*).
This page (from top): Winter buds of a horse chestnut twig; spindle in fruit; crab apple blossom; hawthorn berries.
Contents page (from top): A crack willow; an old pollard hornbeam; an ancient holly tree with berries; a sweet chestnut.

Text copyright © 2002 Hodder Wayland
Volume copyright © 2002 Hodder Wayland

Editor: Polly Goodman
Designer: Mark Whitchurch
Photographer: Archie Miles

Archie Miles gratefully acknowledges the assistance of Westonbirt Arboretum, Gloucestershire; Queenswood Arboretum, Herefordshire; The Foley Estate; Hergest Croft Gardens; Emmy Johnson (planting seedling); Trees for London (urban tree planting).

First published in Great Britain in 2002 by Hodder Wayland, an imprint of Hodder Children's Books.

20550689

British Library Cataloguing in Publication Data
Greenaway, Theresa
    The Hodder Wayland Book of Common British Trees
    1. Trees - Great Britain - Juvenile literature
    2. Trees - Great Britain - Identification - Juvenile literature
    I. Title II. Common British trees
    582.1'6'0941

ISBN 0 7502 3897 6

Printed and bound in Italy by G. Canale & C.Sp.A., Turin

Hodder Children's Books
A division of Hodder Headline Limited
338 Euston Road, London NW1 3BH

Contents

3

What are Trees and Shrubs?

Trees and shrubs are plants with tough, woody stems. In Britain and the rest of the world, there are many thousands of different kinds, or species, of trees. They are very important to people, animals and the environment. Trees can provide us with wood for building, and for making furniture, tools and utensils. Some produce fruits and nuts that people and animals can eat. Animals also use trees for shelter. Birds, bats and squirrels nest in branches or in tree holes.

PARTS OF TREES AND SHRUBS

Trees and shrubs are made up of roots, one or more woody trunks or branches, and fruits that produce many seeds. Roots anchor the tree or shrub into the soil. They also take up water and nutrients that are essential for the tree's growth. Some trees have roots that store food.

WHAT'S THE DIFFERENCE?

Trees can grow to over 5 metres tall. They have a single, woody stem called a trunk, which bears a crown of leafy branches. Shrubs are smaller than trees. Some can grow over 5 metres, although they are never as tall as most trees. Others grow to less than one metre tall. Shrubs do not have one single woody trunk. Instead they have many woody branches on or near the ground.

BROADLEAVED TREES, CONIFERS AND PALMS

Trees are divided into three groups: broadleaved trees, conifer trees and palm trees. Broadleaved trees all have

▶ *Shrubs, like this hazel shrub, have a number of branches that grow from the ground.*

◀ *Trees, like this field oak, have a single trunk topped with a crown of branches.*

flowers. Their seeds are enclosed in fruits. Many, but not all broadleaved trees have broad, flat leaves.

Conifers do not have flowers. Instead, their seeds grow in woody or fleshy cones, or simply sit in a soft, juicy cup. The leaves of conifers are often hard, narrow 'needles'.

Palm trees also have flowers. They have a single, woody trunk with a cluster of very large leaves right at the top.

Broadleaved trees and conifers grow in Britain and the rest of Europe, but the majority of palm trees can only grow in the warmer, tropical regions of the world.

▼ *Broadleaved trees have flowers and seeds enclosed in fruits. Most broadleaved trees are deciduous.*

▼ *Conifer trees, like these Scots pines, have woody or fleshy cones instead of flowers. Most conifers are evergreen.*

▼ *Palm trees, like these palms fringing a beach in Trinidad, have slender trunks and a crown of large leaves.*

EVERGREEN OR DECIDUOUS?

Trees and shrubs that shed all their leaves in the autumn are called deciduous. Trees and shrubs that keep their green leaves throughout the winter are called evergreen. Deciduous trees shed their leaves to avoid the harsh winter weather. Fierce wind, frost and snow would all damage delicate leaves, and leafy branches can be blown down more easily than bare branches. Evergreen trees have tough leaves that do not tear easily, or narrow leaves that let the wind blow through the branches.

Before a deciduous tree or shrub sheds its leaves, many of the nutrients stored in the leaves pass back into the branches. Waste products pass into the dying leaves. These chemical changes make the leaves change colour from green to red, orange, yellow and brown. Some kinds of trees are famous for their brilliant autumn colours.

▲ *The red oak is famous for the deep red colour of its autumn leaves.*

▶ *As this butterfly feeds on the flowers of this buddleia tree it will carry pollen from one flower to another, pollinating the flowers.*

LIFE CYCLE OF A TREE

Trees begin as seeds, which grow into saplings and then adult trees. The seeds of a tree grow in the female part of its flower, or in a female cone. Before a seed can start growing, pollen from the male part of a flower, or from a male cone, has to travel to the female part. This is called pollination. Some trees and shrubs are pollinated by the wind, which blows the pollen from tree to tree. Others are pollinated by insects, such as bees and flies.

HOW SEEDS ARE SPREAD

Trees and shrubs have to make sure their seeds are spread over a wide area, so their saplings do not die from overcrowding. Some use the wind to spread their seeds. Ash and sycamore trees have winged fruits that are caught by the wind. Willows and poplars have seeds covered in masses of cottony hairs that drift through the air. Other kinds of trees use birds to spread their seeds. Birds eat the berries of hawthorn and rowan, and the seeds pass out unharmed in their droppings. The seed pods of laburnum split explosively, flicking their seeds out.

▲ *The wing shape of these field maple fruits help them catch in the wind and disperse the seeds inside.*

▶ *The bright-red colour of these hawthorn berries attract birds, who spread the seeds inside the berries by eating them.*

White willow

Scientific name: *Salix alba*
Height: up to 25 metres
Bark: dark grey, diamond-shaped ridges
Native

Willow trees all prefer damp soil, so the white willow is most likely to be found beside rivers, streams or ponds. The white willow is a graceful tree. Its leaves are long and narrow. White hairs on both sides of the leaves make them look pale bluish-green from above and white from underneath. From a distance, the whole tree looks pale, which is how it got its name. Like all willows, the white willow's tiny flowers are arranged in catkins, which are either male or female. White willow catkins open at the same time as the leaves.

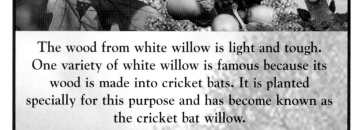

The wood from white willow is light and tough. One variety of white willow is famous because its wood is made into cricket bats. It is planted specially for this purpose and has become known as the cricket bat willow.

▲ *White willows have a tall, billowing crown and pale leaves.*

Weeping willow

Scientific name: *Salix x sepulcralis*
Height: up to 10 metres
Bark: pale greyish-brown, ridged
Hybrid

The weeping willow has very long twigs or shoots, which hang straight down from its curving branches. It is often planted beside ponds, where its graceful shoots with their long, slender leaves almost touch the water.

The weeping willow is a hybrid. This means that it is a cross between two different species of willow tree. One of its parents was a white willow. The other was a willow tree from China, called the Chinese weeping willow. The Chinese tree does not grow very well in Britain, but the hybrid flourishes. New plants are grown from short shoots cut from a plant, called cuttings.

◄ *With its long, hanging twigs, weeping willow is one of the most graceful trees.*

Pussy willow or sallow

Scientific name: *Salix caprea*
Height: up to 10 metres
Bark: smooth, pale grey with small diamond-shaped cracks
Native

This small tree or bushy shrub is one of the first plants to flower in spring, sometimes even in late December or early January. The male catkins of pussy willows have thick, white silky hairs like a cat's soft fur, which is how this tree got its name. When the seed capsules are ripe, they split to release tiny seeds covered in fluffy hairs. Pussy willow leaves are oval and pointed.

▶ *After they have shed their pollen, these male pussy willow catkins will fall from the tree.*

Osier

Scientific name: *Salix viminalis*
Height: up to 6 metres
Bark: greyish-brown, becoming cracked with age
Native

The osier often grows as a dense thicket, in waterlogged ground on marshes, or beside streams and ponds. Its leaves are long and narrow. You can tell the difference between osier leaves and other willow leaves because their edges are rolled under.

◀ *New osier shoots are long and straight, ideal for weaving into baskets.*

Osier, almond and purple willows are used to make baskets. When the willows are cut at ground level, many shoots spring up the following year. The new shoots grow long and straight, often as much as 2.5 metres in a single year. They are woven into many different shapes and sizes of baskets.

Crack willow

Scientific name: *Salix fragilis*
Height: up to 15 metres
Bark: greyish brown, with deep ridges
Native

Like white willows, the crack willow also grows beside rivers and streams. The leaves of this tree are lance-shaped with toothed edges. Although they are a similar shape to white willow leaves, crack willow leaves are larger and darker green. The twigs snap off easily, which is how this tree got its name. When they break off, the twigs float downstream until they lodge in the riverbank. Then they take root and grow into a new tree.

▶ *A crack willow, with its branches hanging in a river.*

If you look closely at ▼ *these male crack willow catkins you can see the long stamens sticking out from each tiny flower.*

Aspen

Scientific name: *Populus tremula*
Height: up to 20 metres
Bark: smooth, greyish-brown
Native

Aspen trees have round-shaped leaves with a wavy edge, each with a long, flattened stalk. The long stalks make the leaves flutter and shake in the breeze. The male and female flowers grow in catkins on separate trees. They appear in spring, well before the leaves have started to open. The male catkins are long and very fluffy.

The aspen is a member of the poplar family. It grows in moist soils and is widespread throughout Britain. It even grows beside streams on mountainsides, but in these

▶ *The leaves of an aspen tree quiver and shake in the breeze.*

▶ *Aspen trees have thin trunks that bend in the wind.*

windswept places, it grows no larger than a small, twiggy bush. In parts of northern Europe and Russia, aspen is an important source of timber.

White poplar

Scientific name: *Populus alba*
Height: up to 20 metres
Bark: smooth, pale grey or white, with rows of diamond-shaped black marks
Introduced

The white poplar was introduced to Britain from Europe. Only female trees will grow in Britain. They grow best in the south of England, and better still in warmer parts of Europe, north Africa and parts of Asia. Thickets of shoots called suckers appear around the base of their trunk.

White poplar leaves vary in size and shape. Some are almost triangular, while others have five large points called lobes. The young leaves are covered with such a dense layer of hairs that the whole leaf is white and soft to touch. As the leaf grows older, these hairs fall from the upper side, and only the underneath stays white.

◀ *White poplars have a pale trunk and young leaves that look almost white because they are covered by white hairs.*

Grey poplar

Scientific name: *Populus x canescens*
Height: over 30 metres
Bark: grey or pale grey, with rows of diamond-shaped black marks
Hybrid

Grey poplars are more common and widespread in Britain than white poplars. The grey poplar is a hybrid between the white poplar and aspen. It is a taller tree than either of its parents. Grey poplar leaves vary in shape. Some look like aspen leaves, while others look more like white poplar leaves.

▼ *These grey poplars have shed their leaves for winter. You can see mistletoe growing on their branches.*

Black poplar

Scientific name: *Populus nigra*
Height: up to 35 metres
Bark: dark, coarsely ridged
Native

The dark bark of the black poplar helps to distinguish it from other poplars. It also has large rough lumps, called burrs, growing on its trunk. Heavy branches grow quite low on its trunk, and it has a broad, spreading crown. The leaves are almost triangular in shape, and male and female catkins grow on separate trees.

The black poplar is now one of Britain's rarest trees, but it was once far more common, growing beside streams and rivers in southern England. It was often planted near farms and villages, because its timber was used to make the bottoms of carts and floorboards. In the 1970s, however, scientists discovered that black poplars had disappeared from many places. They also found that there were no seedlings to replace older trees that had died or had been felled.

There are two main reasons why black poplars have become so rare. The first is because the seeds are small and rely on the silt left behind on flooded riverside meadows to germinate and grow. Farmers have drained many of these meadows to graze their animals on the land, so black poplar seedlings have been unable to grow, or have been eaten by the grazing animals.

▲ *This splendid black poplar is one of Britain's rarest native trees. Hopefully, in the future it will become a common sight again.*

The second reason the black poplar has become rare is because in the past, only trees with catkins of male flowers were planted near houses and farms. Female trees were seldom planted because when the ripe seed capsules split, they release tiny seeds embedded in enormous amounts of fluff. The fluff helps the seeds to be carried away on the breeze, but when it drifts through open windows and doors, it irritates people's noses and eyes. Gradually, the number of female trees dropped, which meant there were fewer new seeds. Efforts are now underway to save the black poplar. Young trees are being cultivated and replanted in places where they used to grow.

Lombardy poplar

Scientific name: *Populus nigra var. italica*
Height: about 30 metres
Bark: greyish brown, ridged, with twigs growing right up the trunk

The Lombardy poplar is a very easy tree to identify. It is a variety of black poplar but instead of heavy, spreading branches, the branches of the Lombardy poplar point stiffly upwards. This creates the tall, narrow crown of the tree. Lombardy poplars are often planted singly in parks for shelter, or in rows to form screens to hide factories.

▶ *Lombardy poplars have a tall, narrow crown with many slender, upswept branches.*

Silver birch

Scientific name: *Betula pendula*
Height: up to 30 metres
Bark: white, with black cracks
Native

The silver birch is a graceful tree, with its 'silver' trunk and slender, drooping twigs. The leaves are small, with toothed edges. The male and female flowers grow in separate catkins on each tree. The female catkins produce many seeds, which are enclosed in dry, winged fruits, which can be carried away by the wind.

Silver birches prefer light, dry soils and are found over much of Britain and Europe. In places where the soil is heavier and wetter, the downy birch is more common. This tree resembles silver birch, but has a grey-green, instead of a white trunk and it has slightly hairy leaves.

> **Bunches of birch twigs tied on to thick sticks make a traditional type of broom, called a besom. This is the broomstick that features in myths and legends, used by witches to fly through the sky. Besoms are still used to sweep garden paths.**

▲ *When the sun shines on silver birch trees, their trunks shine like silver, which is how the tree got its name.*

▶ *Male and female silver birch catkins. The male catkins are bigger and dangle downwards. The female catkins are much smaller and stand stiffly upright.*

Alder

Scientific name: *Alnus glutinosa*
Height: over 25 metres
Bark: greyish-brown, with square-shaped cracks

Like willows and poplars, alders also grow in waterlogged places next to rivers, streams and marshes. They grow close together, their roots helping to bind the soil and prevent it being washed away. The dark-green leaves are round-shaped, with a notch at the tip. Male and female flowers grow on the same tree as separate catkins.

> **In the past, alderwood was used to make waterproof shoes, called clogs. The wood was used to make the whole shoe, or just the sole. Alderwood clogs were carved to fit the owner's foot exactly and were said to be very comfortable.**

▲ *When alder seeds fall off the tree into rivers, their seeds are so light that they float on the surface of the water until they reach somewhere suitable to germinate and grow.*

Hornbeam

Scientific name: *Carpinus betulus*
Height: up to 30 metres
Bark: smooth, mid-grey with vertical brown streaks
Native

The hornbeam is widespread in much of Europe and parts of south-east England. Epping Forest, in Essex, is famous for its hornbeams. In the past, the branches of these trees were cut by Londoners for firewood. Repeated cutting of a tree's branches back to the trunk is called pollarding.

Hornbeam leaves are medium-sized, oval and coarsely toothed. The male and female flowers grow in separate catkins. Each seed grows inside a tiny nut, which has a papery, three-lobed 'wing'. When these winged nuts fall from the tree, the wind carries them and spreads them over a wide area.

▲ *The hornbeam trees of Hatfield Forest, in Essex, have been pollarded for centuries. Local people had the right to use the wood they cut from them for firewood.*

◄ *The hornbeam, like other wind-pollinated trees, has male and female flowers in separate catkins. These catkins are made up of male flowers.*

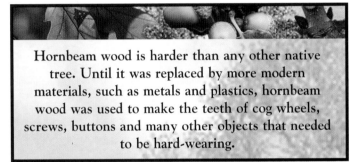

Hornbeam wood is harder than any other native tree. Until it was replaced by more modern materials, such as metals and plastics, hornbeam wood was used to make the teeth of cog wheels, screws, buttons and many other objects that needed to be hard-wearing.

Hazel

Scientific name: *Corylus avellana*
Height: up to 6 metres
Bark: smooth, brown
Native

Hazel is a very common and widespread shrub, with several branched stems. It can grow quite tall but it is often cut back, either because it is in a hedge or because it is used as a source of wood for 'wattle' fencing, hurdles, small poles or firewood. Hazel also produces tasty nuts, which are enjoyed by people, as well as squirrels, mice and voles. Since it is so useful, hazels are often planted. Every seven years or so the shoots are harvested by cutting them at ground level. This practice is known as coppicing. New shoots start to grow the following year.

► *Hazel is one of the most commonly coppiced trees.*

Beech

Scientific name: *Fagus sylvatica*
Height: up to 40 metres
Bark: smooth, grey
Native

Beech forests grow in southern England and mainland Europe. Some of these forests are natural, but others have been planted for their timber. Beech trees grow best in well-drained soil. Their leafy crowns cast shade on the ground below, so few plants are able to grow beneath them except in clearings, where a tree has fallen down.

As the leaves open, clusters of small, greenish, male or female flowers also appear. One or two beech seeds grow as nuts inside a bristly cup, which splits open when the seeds are ripe. Although they are edible, beech nuts are usually too small for people to bother to eat, but plenty are eaten by squirrels, mice and other animals.

Beech trees only produce seeds about once every four years, when a huge crop of seeds will appear. When the seeds start to grow, they carpet the forest floor with fresh green seedlings, but almost all of these will die. Only a few survive to grow into mature beech trees.

Beechwood is fine-grained and hard-wearing. In Buckinghamshire, in the eighteenth and nineteenth centuries, craftsmen set up workshops in the beech woodlands, where they felled the trees and used the timber to make chair legs and other products. These workmen were called 'bodgers'. Beechwood is still used to make furniture, including chairs and sofa frames, as well as kitchen utensils such as rolling pins and wooden spoons.

▲ The beech is one of our best timber trees, but it is also an extremely attractive tree with its grey trunk and spreading branches.

▶ Young beech seedlings starting to cover a forest floor.

Sweet chestnut

Scientific name: *Castanea sativa*
Height: about 30 metres
Bark: brown with spiral ridges
Introduced

The sweet chestnut comes from southern Europe, north Africa and south-west Asia. It was probably introduced to Britain by the Romans, who ground the nuts into a type of flour. Today, chestnuts are either roasted over a fire and eaten as a winter snack, or made into a savoury stuffing for turkey. They can also be used to make rich puddings.

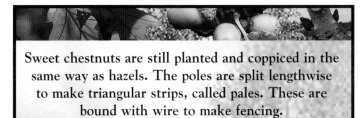

Sweet chestnuts are still planted and coppiced in the same way as hazels. The poles are split lengthwise to make triangular strips, called pales. These are bound with wire to make fencing.

Sweet chestnut leaves are large, lance-shaped and deeply toothed. The smooth brown chestnuts, each of which contains one large seed, are encased inside a husk that is spiny and painful to handle.

▶ *These prickly husks have split open to reveal the shiny, ripe, sweet chestnuts inside.*

▼ *Sweet chestnut trees usually have a broad, spreading crown and bark that grows in spiral ridges around the trunk.*

Holly

Scientific name: *Ilex aquifolium*
Height: up to 25 metres
Bark: smooth, grey with darker marks and small bumps
Native

▲ *Male and female holly flowers grow on separate trees. Only the female flowers develop into berries, which is why some holly trees never have any berries at all – they are male!*

▲ *This ancient holly tree is covered in scarlet berries. These will provide plenty of winter food for wood pigeons, blackbirds and thrushes.*

Holly is the only native broadleaved tree that is evergreen, though some native shrubs such as box also keep their leaves in winter. Holly is one of the easiest trees to identify because the edges of the thick, dark-green leaves are wavy, with each curve ending in a very sharp spine. The spines discourage animals such as deer from eating the leaves. Right at the top of a holly tree, the leaves are not spiny because they are out of animals' reach.

The holly tree's small, white flowers are in separate male or female clusters. They are pollinated by bees and other insects. Bunches of scarlet berries, each containing three or four seeds, ripen in late summer. In autumn and winter, these are eaten by blackbirds, thrushes and redwings, but they are poisonous to humans.

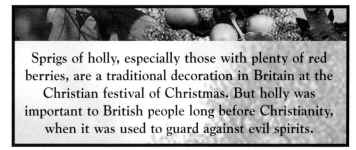

Sprigs of holly, especially those with plenty of red berries, are a traditional decoration in Britain at the Christian festival of Christmas. But holly was important to British people long before Christianity, when it was used to guard against evil spirits.

Common oak

Scientific name: *Quercus robur*
Height: over 30 metres
Bark: dark grey-brown, rough and cracked
Native

Oak makes strong, valuable timber with many uses. In the past, ships were built of oak. Enormous oak timbers were also used to make the framework of houses, barns and other buildings. Other materials such as metal have mostly replaced oak in shipbuilding, but it is still used to make furniture.

Oak forests used to cover large areas of Britain and other parts of Europe. As the human population grew, many of these forests were cleared to make way for farmland and settlements. But oak trees are still very common in parks and gardens, as well as in the remaining woodlands.

There are over 800 different species of oak worldwide, but only two species are native to Britain. The common oak is the most widespread of these, but in the wetter north and west of Britain, sessile oak is more common.

Oak is one of Britain's most familiar and best-loved trees. Its lobed leaves are easy to recognize, as are its fruits – single-seeded acorns about 2 centimetres long that sit in a scaly cup. One of the main differences between common and sessile oaks is that the acorns of the common oak grow on long stalks, whereas the acorns of the sessile oak are stalkless.

Oak trees support an amazing variety of wildlife. Jays and other birds feast on the acorns. They bury some for future meals, but acorns that get forgotten germinate and grow. In this way, birds help the oak tree to spread.

◀ *The stalkless acorns of the sessile oak are packed tightly together. Each fat acorn sits snugly in a cup.*

▼ *The crown of a common oak is broad and spreading when it has grown in an open space. In a wood, close to other oaks, it has a much narrower crown.*

Holm oak

Scientific name: *Quercus ilex*
Height: up to 28 metres
Bark: almost black, cracked into thin squares
Introduced

The holm oak comes from southern Europe and was introduced to Britain around the beginning of the sixteenth century. Unlike the common or sessile oak, the holm oak is evergreen. It has dark-green leaves that are hairy and rough to touch, often silvery underneath. These leaves are not lobed, but the edges and tips sometimes have small spines. The acorns are much smaller (no more than 1.8 centimetres long) and sit more deeply in the cup than those of the common oak.

Holm oaks have been planted in parks, gardens and along riverbanks in south-west England. They are impressive trees that cast a dense shade.

▲ *It has taken many years for this holm oak to develop its broad trunk and magnificent spreading crown.*

► *Holm oak acorns are much smaller than those of the common oak.*

Red oak

Scientific name: *Quercus borealis*
Height: up to 25 metres
Bark: smooth and grey, sometimes with shallow cracks or scattered lumps
Introduced

The red oak came to Britain from eastern North America. It is one of a number of species of oaks that have been brought to Britain from other countries. Some of these will not grow very well in our climate, and many are only seen inside botanical gardens, where they are specially looked after. Of these introduced oaks, the red, scarlet and Turkey oaks are the ones you are most likely to find.

The red oak has large leaves, up to 20 centimetres long, with pointed lobes that are sometimes toothed. In the autumn, these leaves turn bright red, often becoming purple before falling. This bright splash of autumn colour is the reason the red oak is planted as an ornamental tree. In its native eastern North America, the red oak gives a brilliant display of colour each autumn, which is a valuable tourist attraction.

► *Red oak leaves have lobes that end in narrow points. In the autumn, these leaves turn a rich, reddish brown.*

Sycamore

Scientific name: *Acer pseudoplatanus*
Height: up to 35 metres
Bark: smooth, grey with flaking patches
Introduced

Although it is native to central and southern Europe, the sycamore spreads its seeds easily in Britain and is now one of the country's most common trees. The seedlings grow so quickly that they soon cast shade over the seedlings of native trees, starving them of sunlight and making it difficult for them to grow. For this reason, many people do not like sycamores and woodland managers often stop them from spreading too much by cutting them down or removing the saplings.

The leaves of sycamores are medium-to-large in size. Each has five toothed lobes, arranged like fingers on a hand. Several greeny yellow flowers grow on a dangling stem up to 20 centimetres long. The flowers are pollinated by bees. When all the flowers are open, it can seem as though the whole tree is humming from the constant buzz of bees gathering nectar. Sycamore seeds grow in winged fruits. When they fall from the tree, the fruits spin round like the rotor blades of a helicopter, carrying the seeds some distance away.

▲ *Although not always popular in woodlands, when growing in the open like this, on a hot day a sycamore provides welcome shade to people and farm animals.*

◄ *Sycamore flowers are small, with yellowish green petals, but they produce plenty of nectar and are pollinated by bees.*

Sycamore wood is used to make kitchen utensils, furniture and some of the finest violins.

► *Each half of this field maple fruit has just one seed inside a tough layer at the base of the wing.*

Field maple

Scientific name: *Acer campestre*
Height: up to 25 metres
Bark: greyish-brown, with fine cracks and ridges
Native

Like the sycamore, field maple leaves are divided into five lobes, but these leaves are smaller than sycamore leaves. When first unfolded, field maple leaves are pinkish-red, but they soon become green. In the autumn, they give another display of colour, turning deep yellow, then sometimes red or purple.

Field maple only grows on chalky or clay soils, mostly in central, southern and eastern England. It grows along hedgerows and on the edges of woodlands.

◄ *Autumn leaves are often brightly coloured. Field maples are one of our most attractive trees at this time of year.*

Ash

Scientific name: *Fraxinus excelsior*
Height: up to 42 metres
Bark: pale brownish-grey, ridged
Native

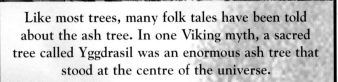

Like most trees, many folk tales have been told about the ash tree. In one Viking myth, a sacred tree called Yggdrasil was an enormous ash tree that stood at the centre of the universe.

Ash trees are some of the last to open their leaves in the spring, and some of the first to shed them as soon as the weather turns cold in the autumn. Each compound leaf is made up of 9–13 small leaflets, arranged in two rows along a central stem, with a single leaflet right at the tip. In the winter, the bare tree is easy to recognize because the black buds show up clearly against the pale-grey twigs. The tree grows small flowers arranged in clusters along the previous year's shoots. They open before the leaves. Each seed is encased in a winged fruit. When they fall, the fruits spin slowly to the ground, or are blown away by the wind.

Ash woodlands are common in the wet, limestone soils of the north of Britain, but ash trees are also scattered across the rest of Britain and Europe.

▶ *A mature ash tree has an uneven, billowing crown.*

▼ *An ash tree is one of the easiest trees to identify in winter. Just look out for these fat buds covered with black bud scales.*

Wood from ash trees is good quality and is used to make many things, including interior woodwork, furniture and wooden kitchen utensils. Ash poles are particularly suitable for walking sticks, and the handles of brooms and other garden tools such as hammers and axes. Since it does not break easily, ash wood is also used for sports equipment such as hockey sticks, billiard cues and oars.

Wild Privet

Scientific name: *Ligustrum vulgare*
Height: up to 3 metres
Bark: dark grey, smooth
Native

Wild privet is a native shrub that grows on chalky soils in England and parts of Europe. It is also planted in gardens, but it is not the same species used in privet hedges, which is called hedging privet.

Wild privet keeps some of its shiny-green, oval leaves throughout the winter. It flowers in the summer, producing small white flowers that are pollinated by insects. Flies in particular are attracted by the unpleasant smell of the flowers. The flowers are followed by bluish-black berries, each of which contains 1–3 seeds. These berries are poisonous to people.

▲ *This wild privet's flowers have just opened, producing a smell that is unpleasant to humans, but probably attractive to insects.*

▲ *In this garden, box has been clipped into neat shapes, surrounded by a yew hedge.*

▶ *Clusters of box flowers grow at the bases of the shiny, dark-green leaves.*

Box

Scientific name: *Buxus sempervirens*
Height: up to 7 metres
Bark: pale brown or grey, cracked into small squares
Native

Box is often shrubby, but it can grow into a small tree. It is found naturally in only a few counties of southern England, on chalky or limy soils. Box gave its name to Box Hill in Surrey, a beauty spot where groves of small box trees grow at the edges of beech woods. Box is also planted in gardens where, like privet it can be clipped into a neat, evergreen hedge.

Box has small, leathery leaves that are dark-green and shiny on top, and a paler, duller colour underneath. The yellow flowers are small and are pollinated by insects. Seeds develop in a round, bluish-green capsule.

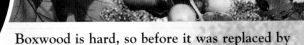

Boxwood is hard, so before it was replaced by other materials such as plastics, it was used to make mathematical instruments such as rulers, and other small items such as pots and pill boxes.

▶ *Wych elms are often seen growing beside farmhouses in northern England and lowland Scotland.*

Wych elm

Scientific name: *Ulmus glabra*
Height: up to 42 metres
Bark: brownish grey, with cracks and furrows
Native

The elm most likely to be seen today, especially in the north and west of Britain, is the wych elm. This tree has a more evenly shaped, spreading crown than the English elm, and its twigs are smooth, not hairy. The wych elm is less susceptible to Dutch elm disease, although it is not immune to it.

◀ *Each oval fruit of wych elm has a broad, papery wing with a single seed in the centre.*

Elmwood has had many uses in the past. Since it is a tough wood that resists splitting, it was used for chair seats, parts of cartwheels, mallet heads and coffins. Wet elm does not rot easily, so it was often the best timber for building structures that were permanently under water. It was also hollowed out to make wooden water pipes. These pipes lasted a surprisingly long time underground, and some have been found over a hundred years after being laid. Elm is still used for flooring, and to make items such as wooden bowls and butchers' blocks.

English elm

Scientific name: *Ulmus procera*
Height: up to 30 metres
Bark: dark brown, cracked into square-shaped plates
Native

The English elm was once one of the most common trees of hedgerows, parks, village greens and farms, growing on deep, fertile soils. Its tall, irregularly shaped crown also made it one of the easiest trees to identify from a distance. Then, in the 1970s, disaster struck. A disease-causing fungus spread by tiny, wood-boring beetles killed elm after elm. In their thousands, the leaves turned brown in mid-summer and the trees died. This was Dutch elm disease. The disease did not originally come from the Netherlands but from Asia, from where it was carried to Europe and North America accidentally on timber. Today, a tree that was once a familiar sight in Britain, with its rough, unevenly shaped leaves and flat, round winged fruits is now an extremely rare sight.

▼ *Underneath the bark of a dead elm, the tell-tale tunnels chewed by the beetles that spread Dutch elm disease are clearly seen.*

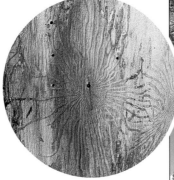

▶ *Mature elms like these were once common in hedgerows, beside playing fields and roads.*

London plane

Scientific name: *Platanus x hispanica*
Height: over 30 metres
Bark: brownish-grey, flakey, with paler patches underneath
Hybrid

The London plane is a cross between the oriental plane from south-east Europe and western Asia, and the American plane. It was first planted in England towards the end of the seventeenth century, and became popular as a street tree in London and other cities because it is able to survive in high levels of atmospheric pollution. Dirt and soot easily wash off its glossy leaves, and its habit of shedding flakes of bark means that dirt clogging the bark is also shed.

Male and female flowers grow in separate, spherical flower heads. Male flowers fall after they have shed their pollen, but the female flower head becomes a round ball of small, seed-containing fruits, which dangle on a long stalk. The leaves are large, about 10 centimetres wide, with five, toothed lobes, arranged like fingers on a hand.

▲ *Since it can tolerate the dirt and grime of London air, the London plane has been planted along some of the capital's busiest roads and in squares in the very heart of the city.*

Common lime

Scientific name: *Tilia x vulgaris*
Height: up to 46 metres
Bark: grey, with ridges and burrs at the base
Hybrid

Common limes are most likely to be found on the edges of pavements in towns and suburbs. However, these street trees give no indication of exactly how large a common lime can grow, because the branches are pruned so that they do not hide street lamps or road signs.

The common lime is a cross between two other native species of lime, the small-leaved lime and the large-leaved lime. Neither of these trees grow as large as the common lime, and they are both quite rare trees in the wild. The small-leaved lime grows scattered among other woodland trees on fertile soils in central England and Wales. The large-leaved lime is also found in England and Wales, but prefers chalky soils.

Lime leaves are heart-shaped and have toothed edges. The flowers smell very sweet and are pollinated by bees.

▲ *Lime trees like these were often planted along the drives leading up to a stately home. This avenue of limes in Clumber Park, Nottingham, is a fine example.*

The fruits are small, hard nuts that hang below a papery, leaf-like bract, which helps to disperse the seeds.

Horse chestnut

Scientific name: *Aesculus hippocastanum*
Height: up to 39 metres
Bark: dark-grey, cracking into rough plates
Introduced

◀ *Freshly fallen, shiny brown conkers.*

▼ *As the sticky bud scales fall from the winter buds of a horse chestnut twig, fresh green leaves unfold and grow.*

The horse chestnut is a magnificent tree, with a short trunk, a broad, spreading crown and very distinctive leaves. Each compound leaf is made up of 5–7 leaflets, which grow like fingers from the tip of the leaf stalk. In May, after the leaves have opened, many spikes of pink-blotched white flowers appear. These look a little like thick candles scattered over the crown of the tree.

Even though it is now such a feature of the British countryside, the horse chestnut is not a native. It originally came from the Balkans, in south-east Europe. The horse chestnut arrived in England in 1629, and has been planted in parks, large gardens and other open spaces. Its large leaves cast a welcome shade on hot summer days, enjoyed by both people and animals.

The wood from horse chestnut is brittle and not very strong. It is made into various small items such as toys, boxes and brush handles.

▲ *A horse chestnut tree in flower is an impressive sight.*

The horse chestnut is most famous for its seeds, the fat, shiny, brown conkers. These grow inside fleshy, spiny fruits, which split when they hit the ground. The conkers are used in a game, where the conkers are threaded with pieces of string. Each contestant takes a conker and swings it at their opponent's conker to try and break it. The winner has the toughest, hardest conker. Some people take these contests very seriously, devising many ways of hardening their conkers, including soaking them in vinegar and slowly heating them in an oven.

Hawthorn

Scientific name: *Crataegus monogyna* and *Crataegus laevigata*
Height: about 10 metres
Bark: dark-brown, cracked into narrow rectangles
Native

There are two kinds of hawthorn that are native to Britain. Both are usually just called hawthorn, although one is more correctly called midland hawthorn. But these two species cross so easily with each other that many of those seen are hybrids.

Hawthorn is one of the most widespread and abundant woody plants of Britain. In a good position it can grow into a small tree, but on an exposed hillside, it will be no more than a gnarled shrub only a few centimetres high. The midland hawthorn prefers the heavy soils and shady woods of central and south-east England, but it has been planted outside this region.

Hawthorns have sharp thorns on their stems. They have small, dark-green leaves divided into lobes. Midland hawthorn leaves are less deeply lobed than those of the more common hawthorn. Both have flat sprays of white or pinkish flowers, which open in May or June. Red berries ripen in the autumn. These contain one or two hard seeds. Blackbirds, thrushes and other birds eat these berries, so by the winter, they have all disappeared.

▲ *Hawthorn usually flowers in May each year.*

◀ *Bright-red berries, called 'haws', cover the branches of hawthorn in September. They are soon eaten by hungry birds and mice.*

Another name for hawthorn is 'May', because this is the month when it is in full flower. There is an English superstition that it is unlucky to take May-blossom indoors.

Rowan

Scientific name: *Sorbus aucuparia*
Height: up to 18 metres
Bark: pale greyish-brown, scaly
Native

Rowan, sometimes called mountain ash, is a small tree that is widespread and common throughout Britain and Europe. In Scotland, it grows higher up the mountainsides than any other tree. Since it is small and attractive, rowan is a popular ornamental tree in gardens.

Its compound leaves have 9–15 leaflets arranged in two rows, with a single leaflet at the tip. Each leaflet is oblong in shape, with toothed edges. In May, flat flower heads of many creamy-white flowers appear, followed by orange-red berries. These ripen in August, and are usually all eaten by birds by the end of the month. The berries can also be eaten by humans, in a sharp-flavoured jelly.

◀ *Rowan is a hardy tree, able to flourish among rocks on mountain slopes as well as in the milder lowlands. Its orange-red berries ripen in August.*

◀ *Each flower head of rowan is a cushion-like mass of small flowers.*

Blackthorn

Scientific name: *Prunus spinosa*
Height: up to 4 metres
Bark: nearly black
Native

Blackthorn is a shrub that spreads by means of suckers – shoots that grow up from the roots often at some distance from the main crown of the plant. Using this method, just one bush of blackthorn can eventually make a large, dense thicket of spiny stems.

The white flowers start to open as early as March, before the leaves. In autumn, blue-black berries called sloes appear. These look as if they have a fine, white sheen. This is called a 'bloom'. It is caused by tiny particles of wax made by the skin of the sloe. Although not poisonous, the thin flesh of the sloe berry is so sour that it is almost impossible to eat.

◀ *Not even birds will eat these purple blackthorn sloes until the frost has softened and sweetened them a little.*

▼ *Blackthorn can quickly grow into a dense thicket, using suckers, or shoots that spread around the main plant.*

Crab apple

Scientific name: *Malus sylvestris*
Height: up to 10 metres
Bark: greyish-brown, scaly
Native

Anyone who has bitten into a crab apple knows just how sour these small apples are, even if they look ripe and rosy! Yet crab apples are the ancestors of much sweeter and juicier eating apples. The first cultivated apples probably came from the Turkestan region of Asia, but today apples are grown all round the world. There are now at least 6,000 varieties of cultivated apple.

Crab apple trees grow mostly at the edges of woods, or in hedgerows and other lightly wooded places. The twigs are often spiny and the leaves are oval. Each flower has five white petals flushed with pink. The fruits (the apples) look like eating apples, but are much smaller, usually no more than 3 centimetres across. The seeds (the pips) are in a core at the centre of the apple. These fruits can grow in large numbers, weighing down the branches of this small tree.

▲ *Crab apple is a common tree in hedgerows, but it can be easy to miss unless it is covered with blossom in spring or weighed down with crab apples in the autumn.*

◀ *Crab apple blossom opens at the same time as the fresh green leaves. The flowers are pollinated by bees.*

Cherry laurel

Scientific name: *Prunus laurocerasus*
Height: up to 10 metres
Bark: dark, slightly rough
Introduced

Cherry laurel is often used in garden hedges and is a popular ornamental plant in shrubberies. It is a fast-growing evergreen and sprouts freely from all stems after being clipped or pruned. It is usually a thick shrub, but may grow into a tree.

Cherry laurel reproduces easily from seeds, so it will quickly spread across gardens or woodlands unless kept under control. It is native to south-east Europe and south-west Asia, and was probably brought to Britain in the sixteenth or seventeenth century.

The cherry laurel's oblong leaves are thick and leathery. They are dark-green and glossy on top and a paler, duller colour underneath. From April to June, the spikes of small

▲ *Little can grow beneath a cherry laurel because the large, glossy, evergreen leaves shade out almost all the light.*

white flowers appear, which are pollinated by insects. Purple-black berries ripen in late summer and are eaten by birds. Both the leaves and the seeds of the cherry laurel are poisonous. They can kill livestock and people if they are eaten in any quantity.

Whitebeam

Scientific name: *Sorbus aria*
Height: up to 23 metres
Bark: grey, developing shallow scales
Native

The whitebeam is a small, attractive tree whose light-green leaves often stand out against the darker leaves of neighbouring trees. The leaves are oval and edged with rounded teeth. The whole leaf appears very pale when it first opens because it is covered with white hairs. The hairs are mostly shed from the upper surface as the leaf matures, but the underside keeps its cottony white coat. It has flower heads of white flowers and berries that turn bright-red in September.

The whitebeam prefers chalky, limy or sandy soils and can be found in the wild in parts of southern Britain and Ireland, and in central and southern Europe. It varies in appearance, differing in the shape and size of its leaves, and the size and colour of its fruit.

▲ *The whitebeam's red berries cling to the tree long after the leaves have fallen in the autumn.*

◄ *The pale-green leaves of the whitebeam are very attractive, especially when it grows next to trees with contrasting, darker-green leaves.*

Wild cherry

Scientific name: *Prunus avium*
Height: up to 31 metres
Bark: purplish, developing black cracks
Native

Although the trunk of a wild cherry tree does not often grow very large, the wood is good quality and is an attractive colour. It is pale when first cut, but darkens to a deep, reddish colour. This means that wild cherry wood is highly prized for making musical instruments, veneers, and crafts such as marquetry.

The wild cherry tree grows in hedgerows, copses and on the edges of woods throughout Britain. It is also planted in parks and gardens. The leaves are sharply toothed and roughly oval in shape. Each white flower grows on a stalk and the flowers are arranged in clusters along the shoots. The fruits (cherries) turn from yellow to dark-red as they ripen. Each cherry has a layer of juicy, acid flesh surrounding a single woody stone, which contains a single seed. Wild cherries are too sharp for human taste, but modern varieties of sweet cherries have all descended from this wild species.

◀ *The wild cherry is usually a tall, slender tree, but this magnificent old tree from Huntley, Gloucestershire shows just how large the wild cherry tree can grow in the open.*

Common or wild pear

Scientific name: *Pyrus communis*
Height: up to 20 metres
Bark: dark-brown or black, deeply cracked into small squares
Introduced

The leaves of common pear trees are oval-shaped and shiny, with finely toothed edges. Their white flowers attract bees and other insects. The pears are small, but they are sweet enough to eat. The flesh of pears contains small, almost gritty particles, called stone cells. Like apples, the black seeds (the pips) are arranged inside a core.

The common pear is the tree from which cultivated pears have been bred. Although it grows wild in hedgerows and waste ground, it is not native to Britain. These wild pear trees have grown from seeds that came from pears in gardens and orchards. There are three groups of cultivated pears: dessert pears that can be eaten raw, cooking pears and perry pears.

Most people are familiar with cider, an alcoholic drink made from apples, but fewer are aware that a similar drink to cider, called perry, can be made from pears. There are at least fourteen different varieties of perry pears, which are grown in orchards. The fruit is picked in autumn, and crushed in a press to remove the juice. The juice is fermented and made into a sparkling drink.

▶ *The pears from the perry pear tree are used to make perry, an alcoholic drink similar to cider.*

Spindle

Scientific name: *Euonymus europaeus*
Height: 5–8 metres
Bark: grey, smooth
Native

Spindle can grow into a small tree, but it is common as a branching shrub in a hedgerow. Spindle is widespread on chalky soils in Britain and many parts of Europe. The leaves are narrow, almost oval and pointed at the tip. They turn red in the autumn. Spindle flowers are no more than 1 centimetre wide, each with four greenish petals. The fruits are much more noticeable. They have four brilliant-pink lobes which split apart when ripe to reveal four bright-orange seeds. Both the seeds and the fruits are poisonous.

▶ *Unlike its flowers, spindle's bright-pink fruits and orange seeds are easy to spot.*

▲ *Spindle's tiny green flowers are easy to miss.*

Guelder rose

Scientific name: *Viburnum opulus*
Height: up to 4 metres
Bark: grey
Native

This shrub is found in woods, hedges and any patches of uncultivated land with damp soil. It is also planted in gardens, where its small size, clusters of white, fragrant flowers and red, translucent fruits make it an attractive addition to a shrubbery. The lobed leaves turn red in the autumn. The flower heads are made up of many flowers, growing in a rounded spray. The outer flowers have much larger petals than the inner flower, but it is only the small, inner flowers that produce red fruits. The fruits are not poisonous, but they do not taste very nice.

The wayfaring tree is a close relative of the guelder rose, but the tree is more restricted to chalky soils in the southern half of Britain. It has dull-green, wrinkled leaves with finely toothed edges. All the small, white flowers produce red fruits that turn purple-black when they are ripe.

◀ *Only the small flowers in the centre of this guelder rose flower head produce fruits.*

Buckthorn

Scientific name: *Rhamnus cathartica*
Height: up to 8 metres
Bark: split, scaly, tinged orange
Native

▶ *As its name suggests, buckthorn branches are armed with sharp thorns.*

Buckthorn is a thorny shrub that grows in hedgerows and open woodlands. It is a common shrub of chalky soils. Buckthorn has oval, pointed leaves that grow opposite each other up the stem. The stems are often thorny. The yellowish-green flowers grow in clusters. The flowers are tiny, but they smell so strongly of honey that they attract many honeybees, which arrive to collect their nectar and pollinate them. After the flowers come the fruits, which are slightly flattened, purplish-black berries. Each berry contains between two and four seeds.

The berries and bark of buckthorn are poisonous. They were once used as a laxative to cure constipation, but their effect is violent, causing sickness, diarrhoea and severe pain, so they are no longer used.

Dogwood

Scientific name: *Cornus sanguinea*
Height: up to 4 metres
Bark: dark-red at first, becoming brown with age
Native

Although not related to the buckthorn, dogwood is also a shrub with oval, pointed leaves arranged opposite each other along the stems. It also has purplish-black fruits, but these are not berries – they are single-seeded fruits with a slightly rough skin. Dogwood flowers are small with white petals. They are arranged in rounded clusters at the tips of the shoots. The fruits are slightly poisonous and have a bitter taste.

Dogwood grows wild in hedges and woodlands, and is common in places where the soil is chalky or limy clay. It is often planted in gardens because in their first winter, the bare twigs are a deep-red colour that provide a welcome splash of colour. Every spring, gardeners cut off these twigs at ground level, so the shrub grows a new set of shoots the following winter to liven up the appearance of the garden.

▲ *Dogwood is a shrub that grows in hedgerows or along the edges of woods.*

◀ *The small white flowers of dogwood attract flies and bees, which pollinate them.*

Rhododendron

Scientific name: *Rhododendron ponticum*
Height: up to 5 metres
Bark: brown, becoming cracked with age
Introduced

Rhododendron is a broad, spreading, evergreen shrub. Its leaves are leathery, oblong and narrow at both ends. The large, domed flower heads consist of many bell-shaped, pinkish flowers, each 5 centimetres wide.

This rhododendron, like many other species of rhododendron, was brought to Britain as an ornamental shrub for parks and gardens. Unfortunately, on acid, peaty or sandy soils, this particular species does so well that it spreads rapidly, both by seeds and by suckers. Banks of rhododendron now grow well along the wet hillsides of Wales and parts of Scotland, as well as on heathlands and in acid woods elsewhere in Britain. Native plants die in the rhododendron's shade, so although in flower it is an impressive sight, the shrub is really a pest that is very hard to control. All parts of the rhododendron are poisonous.

▲ *Rhododendron's bright pink flowers are a pretty sight, but this shrub can be a ruthless pest.*

Elder

Scientific name: *Sambucus nigra*
Height: up to 10 metres
Bark: brownish-grey, furrowed and cork
Native

The elder is one of our most familiar hedgerow plants, where it grows into a shrub or possibly a small tree. The leaves are compound, with 3–7 leaflets. You can pick it out easily on any journey across the countryside in June or July, because its large, flat flower heads made up of many small, creamy white flowers are unmistakeable, even from the window of a car or train. These flowers have a sweet, strong fragrance and are used to make sparkly but non-alcoholic, elderflower 'champagne'.

By late summer, the purple-black fruits are ripe. Eating quantities of the raw fruit is likely to make you feel a bit sick, but elderberry wine can be excellent.

▶ *If you want to make elderberries into wine or syrup, you will have to pick them before the birds eat them!*

▲ *Elder flowers have a strong, sweet smell.*

Gorse

Scientific name: *Ulex europaeus*
Height: up to 2.5 metres
Bark: greyish
Native

Gorse is a prickly shrub, with each stem covered with branched, bluish-green spines. Only young gorse plants have leaves. As the plant gets older, the leaves are replaced by scales or more spines. The seeds develop in black pods, which can be heard splitting in hot sunshine. The flowers are bright-yellow mostly open in June, although it is possible to find gorse flowers at any month of the year. A bank of gorse in full flower smells strongly of coconut.

◀ In order to pollinate these gorse flowers, insects have to climb right into each blossom.

▼ The best place to find gorse is on a dry, sandy heath.

Broom

Scientific name: *Cytisus scoparius*
Height: up to 2.5 metres
Bark: green, ridged
Native

Broom is an upright shrub in the same family as gorse, but it does not have any spines. Each leaf is made up of three small leaflets. The flowers are yellow, with red or mauve patches. Like gorse, the fruits are black pods that split open explosively, shooting out the ripe seeds.

▲ Broom flowers are yellow, with red or mauve patches.

◀ Broom is very similar to gorse, but it does not have sharp spines.

29

Laburnum

Scientific name: *Laburnum anagyroides*
Height: up to 8 metres
Bark: smooth, dark-green, becoming brown
Introduced

Laburnum is a small, deciduous tree which is well-suited to gardens of all sizes. It was introduced from the mountains of central and southern Europe in 1560. Since then it has been planted in Britain and other parts of Western Europe. The young shoots and buds are silky with grey hairs. The compound leaves, which are divided into three leaflets, are also covered with silvery-grey hairs underneath. In late

◀ *The laburnum is one of the best trees to have in a small garden. It does not grow too tall, and every year it produces cascades of yellow flowers.*

May, the whole tree is transformed when the hanging spikes of bright-yellow flowers appear. Laburnum is poisonous and the seeds could cause serious illness if eaten.

▲ *The branches of a walnut tree often grow low down on the trunk, making them a cool, leafy place to sit on a hot summer's day.*

Walnut

Scientific name: *Juglans regia*
Height: up to 24 metres
Bark: pale-grey and smooth, with widely spaced cracks
Introduced

The walnut tree was introduced to Britain and Western Europe in the sixteenth century, and since then it has been planted both for its edible seeds, the walnuts, and for its valuable timber. It is native to an area from south-east Europe to south-west China. Walnut has very long, compound leaves up to 40 centimetres in length, with 3–9 leaflets. Male flowers grow in a catkin, but each greenish female flower grows at the tip of a young shoot. The fruit has a fleshy green outer layer surrounding a hard, woody stone, inside which is the walnut.

Cider gum or Eucalyptus

Scientific name: *Eucalyptus gunnii*
Height: up to 30 metres
Bark: peeling in strips of pinkish-brown, smooth-grey underneath
Introduced

▶ *The eucalyptus, or gum tree is easy to recognize from its bluish-green leaves and peeling, stringy bark.*

There are over 500 different kinds of eucalyptus, or gum trees, in Australia, but very few are hardy enough to survive in the British climate. The evergreen cider gum is the toughest, and is sometimes seen in our parks and gardens. Its young leaves are used in floral arrangements. These young leaves are round, stalkless and grow opposite each other in pairs up the stem. They are a distinctive, pale bluish-grey. The leaves on older branches are spear-shaped and darker in colour.

Magnolia

Scientific name: *Magnolia x soulangiana*
Height: up to 7.5 metres
Bark: blackish-grey
Hybrid

◀ *Anyone with magnolia trees like these in their garden hopes that the weather stays mild when the flowers are out. Frost kills the flowers and turns them brown.*

The magnolia is a small tree or shrub with large, attractive flowers. The species named above is a hybrid and is common in gardens, but there are about thirty-five other species of magnolia, which come from Asia and North America. Gardeners in Britain and Europe like the magnolia because of its large flowers.

Unfortunately, many of the flowers open early in the year. If there is a frost, all the flowers are killed. The bull bay is an evergreen magnolia tree from south-eastern North America, which is often planted against sunny walls in southern England. Its waxy, petalled flowers have a strong, sweet smell.

Butterfly bush or Buddleia

Scientific name: *Buddleia davidii*
Height: up to 5 metres
Bark: grey
Introduced

▶ *Butterflies of many different kinds are attracted to the nectar-rich buddleia flowers.*

This shrub is very popular with butterflies, which is how it got one of its names. Butterflies are attracted to its spikes of small, but highly scented mauve flowers. It has bluish-green, lance-shaped leaves, some of which cling to the stems all year round, but most fall, so it is only semi-evergreen. The butterfly bush spreads its seeds freely in open spaces and will colonize the most inhospitable sites alongside railway lines or on wasteland. It originally came from China.

Common juniper

Scientific name: *Juniperus communis*
Height: up to 10 metres
Bark: reddish-brown, shredding
Native

Common juniper seldom reaches its full height in Britain, and is usually a low-growing, spreading shrub. It is one Britain's three native conifers. Common juniper has short, narrow leaves arranged in whorls of three. On junipers found on chalky and limy areas of southern Britain, these needles are stiff and sharp. But on the junipers found on the higher ground of northern England, Scotland and north-west Wales, the needles are much softer. Common juniper has small, round cones no more than 1 centimetre across. Each cone contains 1–6 seeds protected within a few fleshy scales. The scales have a pleasant, aromatic smell when crushed.

▲ *Juniper can survive harsh weather conditions on high mountain slopes. The trunk is tough, gnarled and contorted into strange shapes by the wind.*

▲ *These juniper 'berries' are really small, fleshy cones. They take three years to ripen.*

▲ *Yew seeds are each enclosed in a fleshy pink cup.*

▶ *This ancient yew tree, which is still growing in Powys, Wales, is mentioned in the Domesday Book. It is thought to be at least 2,000 years old.*

Yew

Scientific name: *Taxus baccata*
Height: up to 28 metres
Bark: scaly, patches of reddish-brown and purplish-brown
Native

Yew is one of Britain's few native evergreen trees. It is usually called a conifer, even though instead of a woody cone, each seed sits in a fleshy pink cup that botanists call an aril. The leaves are flat and narrow, coloured dark-green above, with two paler lines underneath. Yew sometimes grows into an upright tree with a single trunk, but weather-beaten yews that grow very slowly, often over hundreds of years, often develop a leaning trunk, low branches or even a number of trunks.

The famous yew forest at Kingley Vale, Hampshire is a nature reserve. Covering the chalk slopes, the sombre yew trees cast a deep shade. Whitebeam trees grow scattered amongst the yew, their pale leaves contrasting with the dark-green leaves of the yew.

There is lots of folklore and superstition attached to yew, going back thousands of years. It has had a long association with churches because it was often planted in graveyards. Yews were planted beside homesteads and farms to protect people from harm. They were also thought to symbolize death, perhaps because the leaves, seeds or bark cause death if eaten.

Yew wood is hard and long-lasting. It has a deep, red-brown colour and an attractive grain, so it is still valued for carving and for quality furniture. It was an important wood for archers in the Middle Ages because its elasticity and resistance to splitting made it ideal for the English longbow, which was made from strips of wood cleaved from a long, straight trunk of yew.

Scots pine

Scientific name: *Pinus sylvestis*
Height: up to 36 metres
Bark: lower trunk: grey and scaly; upper trunk: light-orange or pinkish
Native

There are over 80 different species of pine trees worldwide, almost all of which are from the northern hemisphere. Of these, many have been brought to Britain and Europe. There are three groups of pines, with needles in bunches of either twos, threes or fives.

Like most conifers, the Scots pine is an evergreen tree. In Britain, it grows naturally in the Scottish highlands, but it has been planted in many other areas to decorate parks and gardens, and for its timber. Scots pine leaves are blue-green needles, 2–8 centimetres long, with a distinct twist. The needles are arranged in pairs. Winged seeds grow inside cones, and take two years to ripen. The ripe cones are woody and greyish brown, measuring between 2.5–6 centimetres long. The Scots pine seeds itself easily in places with a light, sandy soil.

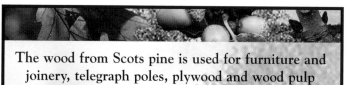

The wood from Scots pine is used for furniture and joinery, telegraph poles, plywood and wood pulp for paper.

▲ *The trunk of a Scots pine is grey near the base, but higher up it is a rust-red colour.*

Austrian pine

Scientific name: *Pinus nigra*
Height: up to 42 metres
Bark: blackish-brown, ridged and scaly
Introduced

This tall, evergreen tree is often planted for its ornamental value, or as a shelter belt – a line of trees that shields property and fields of crops from the wind. Unlike many conifers, it will grow on chalky soils. Austrian pine looks dark in appearance with its almost-black trunk and dark-green leaves. The needles are 8–12 centimetres long and like those of the Scots pine, are arranged in pairs. The woody cones are similar in appearance to those of the Scots pine, broad at the base and tapering to a point, but they are a little larger, measuring 5–7.5 centimetres long.

◄ *The cones of this Austrian pine are waiting for a hot sunny day, which will make them crack open and release their winged seeds.*

Norway spruce

Scientific name: *Picea abies*
Height: up to 46 metres
Bark: reddish-brown becoming purplish, cracked into small plates
Introduced

Spruces have much shorter, stiffer needles than pines. Their cones are less hard and woody than pine cones, and they are more cylindrical in shape. Just like pine cones, when they are ripe, spruce cones open to release small, winged seeds. The fast-growing Norway spruce is the tree most often used as a Christmas tree in Europe and North America. Even when it grows tall, it keeps its typical, Christmas-tree shape, with dense whorls of branches growing low on the trunk and a crown that tapers to a point. The needles are just 1–2 centimetres long, ending in a point. Each needle stays on the tree for 5–7 years.

▶ *New shoots and needles of a Norway spruce.*

Silver fir from Europe, and grand and noble fir from North America, are gaining popularity as Christmas trees in Britain because they do not shed their needles so easily. Blue spruce also makes a very pretty Christmas tree, but the pale-bluish-green needles are very stiff and sharply pointed. It also grows slowly, which makes it an expensive alternative to the Norway spruce.

The habit of bringing a tree into the house and decorating it for Christmas was not practised in Britain until Queen Victoria's husband, Prince Albert, introduced the custom from his native Germany in the nineteenth century. It was such a popular idea that it soon became a firmly established part of the Christmas tradition in Britain, North America and many other countries.

▲ *This tall Norway spruce shows what a Christmas tree could look like if it was allowed to grow.*

Larch

Scientific name: *Larix decidua*
Height: up to 46 metres
Bark: greenish-grey, smooth, becoming cracked
Introduced

Larch trees have narrow, cone-shaped crowns and twigs that droop down from whorled branches, giving the tree a graceful appearance. The larch is one of the few conifers that is deciduous. In the autumn, the narrow leaves turn golden-yellow and fall. The small, egg-shaped cones are bright pinkish-red at first, but they turn brown when they are ripe. These colourful young cones are sometimes called larch 'roses', but unlike flowers, they have soft scales instead of petals. The cones ripen in one year but often remain on the tree for much longer, even after all their seeds have blown away.

▲ *Larch trees are one of just a few conifers that shed their leaves in autumn.*

The larch is frequently grown in plantations for its timber. The wood has many uses, especially for outdoor joinery and woodwork.

▲ *The young female cones of the larch are such a bright-pink colour that they are sometimes called larch 'roses'.*

Douglas fir

▶ *The Douglas fir is one of the largest timber trees in the world.*

▼ *Douglas fir cones hang down beneath the leafy shoots.*

Scientific name: *Pseudotsuga menziesii*
Height: up to 58 metres
Bark: purplish-black, with deep, brown cracks
Introduced

Douglas fir comes from the west coast of North America, where the tallest tree ever felled measured an amazing 117 metres. It will not grow quite that tall in Britain, but it does reach an impressive size. The needles are soft and bright-green, with two white bands underneath. If the leaves are crushed, they give off a sweet smell of sticky resin. Douglas fir cones are unlike those of any other conifer. Each woody scale has a three-pronged, papery bract on its outer surface.

In the past, the Douglas fir's tall, straight trunk has been used for the masts of sailing ships. Today, Douglas fir timber harvested from plantations in many countries is used for veneers, plywood and construction work. It is also planted in parks and large gardens for decoration.

Cedar of Lebanon

Scientific name: *Cedrus libani*
Height: up to 40 metres
Bark: dark-grey, with small, scaly ridges and short cracks
Introduced

The cedar of Lebanon came from the Middle East. It is a stately tree often planted on the sweeping lawns of large, country houses. Huge branches arch out from low on the trunk. Towards the middle of these heavy branches, dense, flat 'plates' of leaves grow on the smaller branches and shoots. Unfortunately, these massive branches are often wrenched off by strong winds. The leaves are dark-green needles that grow in whorls, and the cones are smooth and egg-shaped. The cones are covered by a sticky white resin, which smells pleasant but is difficult to wipe off your fingers. The resin is the tree's way of defending itself against insect attack. Cedar cones sometimes fall from the

▲ *The broad, spreading crown of the cedar of Lebanon needs plenty of space to reach its full size.*

tree whole, but they often break up while they are still attached to the tree so you may only find scattered woody scales on the ground below.

Atlas cedar

Scientific name: *Cedrus atlantica*
Height: up to 39 metres
Bark: dark-grey, cracked into large plates
Introduced

▶ *Like all cedars, Atlas cedar cones are made up of overlapping scales, and grow straight up on the branches.*

Atlas cedars come from the Atlas mountains of North Africa. One variety, with blue-green leaves, is often planted in large gardens, churchyards and other public places. Atlas cedars are very attractive trees, but anyone wishing to plant this or any other cedar must remember that cedars can grow very large.

Deodar cedar

Scientific name: *Cedrus deodara*
Height: up to 37 metres
Bark: brownish-grey, cracked into small plates
Introduced

This cedar comes from the Himalayan mountains. It is different from the Atlas cedar because the tips of its shoots always droop slightly. The needles, which can grow up to 5 centimetres long, are slightly longer than those of the Atlas cedar. When it is young, the whole tree has a silvery appearance because soft hairs cover the shoots.

◀ *The deodar cedar, like many other cedars, is an attractive tree often planted on large lawns.*

Lawson's cypress

Scientific name: *Chamaecyparis lawsoniana*
Height: up to 41 metres
Bark: purplish-brown, flaky
Introduced

Lawson's cypress comes from the western North America. It grows into a very tall tree with a flame-shaped crown and branches growing often right down to the ground, hiding most of the trunk. The leaves of this and other cypresses are like green scales that are pressed closely to the shoots, often making a flattened spray. When the bark is damaged, sticky resin oozes from the wound. Cypress cones are spherical. They are much smaller than those of pines or spruces, and have only a few scales, each with a point or small lump in the centre. When the cones are ripe, a large number of small, winged seeds are released.

▲ *Lawson's cypress has a flame-shaped crown and branches that grow low on the trunk.*

▶ *The cones of Lawson's cypress are less than 1 centimetre wide and have just eight scales.*

Leyland cypress

Scientific name: *x Cupressocyparis leylandii*
Height: up to 34 metres
Bark: reddish-brown, shallow cracks
Hybrid

The Leyland cypress grows leaves in flattened, fan-shaped sprays. Its shiny cones are about 2.5 centimetres wide. Leyland cypress is a hybrid between two other kinds of cypress: one from California and one that grows from Alaska down through western Canada to Oregon. The hybrid was produced by chance when two of these trees were planted close together in Wales in the nineteenth century. It quickly became very popular as a fast-growing wind shield. However, this conifer has caused more disputes between neighbours than any other tree. Young Leyland cypresses are frequently planted as a hedge around gardens. If it is allowed to grow untrimmed, it soon forms a very high, dense bank of leaves that casts a deep shade over neighbours' houses and gardens.

◀ *The Leyland cypress can be grown into a useful windbreak.*

Monterey cypress

Scientific name: *Cupressus macrocarpa*
Height: up to 37 metres
Bark: brown and ridged
Introduced

Monterey cypress comes from the windswept Monterey Bay, in California, so it is not surprising that this tree flourishes near the coasts of southern England, forming gnarled hedges. Inland it grows much taller and straighter, and it is often planted in parks and other public areas for decoration. The small, scale-like leaves grow on bushy shoots that are not flattened into sprays. The cones are about 4 centimetres wide. Like almost all other conifers, the pollen-producing male cones grow on the same tree as the seed-producing female cones. With age, the crown of Monterey cypress becomes irregular and spreading.

▶ *This Monterey cypress is tall, because it is growing inland. Near the coast, it grows as small hedges.*

Wellingtonia

Scientific name: *Sequoiadendron giganteum*
Height: up to 50 metres
Bark: reddish-brown, very thick, spongy and fibrous
Introduced

◀ *The wellingtonia's cones are about 7.5 centimetres long, egg-shaped and knobbly.*

The wellingtonias of California are the biggest, though not quite the tallest trees in the world. Some of these trees are thought to be over 2,000 years old and have an estimated weight of over 2,000 tonnes. The first wellingtonias were brought to Britain in 1853, so the oldest trees are less than 200 years old. They are often planted as a landscape feature in country estates.

Wellingtonia has bright-green, scale-like leaves, but the points of each leaf stick out, making the shoot feel spiky if you run your hand along it from tip to base. The extremely thick, fibrous bark protects the trunk from the forest fires that are a natural feature of its Californian environment.

▶ *The wellingtonia needs lots of space in parks or arboreta because it grows so tall, but in its native North America, it grows even taller.*

Ginkgo

Scientific name: *Ginkgo biloba*
Height: up to 30 metres
Bark: brown, corky, becoming cracked and ridged
Introduced

The ginkgo, or maidenhair tree, is the only survivor of a family of trees that flourished 150–200 million years ago. This family was once widespread over the northern hemisphere, but today, wild ginkgo only survives on the Tianmu Mountains of China. In Britain, it is planted in parks and gardens.

Ginkgo leaves are fan-shaped and split into two lobes. The veins of the leaf look like the 'spokes' of the fan. Ginkgo has neither flowers nor cones. The pollen organs grow on a kind of catkin. The female, seed-producing organs grow in clusters at the ends of short shoots. There are separate male and female trees.

▲ *Ginkgo trees are deciduous. The leaves of this tree are starting to turn yellow in the autumn.*

Monkey puzzle

Scientific name: *Araucaria araucana*
Height: up to 29 metres
Bark: grey, wrinkled into bands, with circular scars where branches have fallen off
Introduced

The monkey puzzle tree comes from the slopes of the Andes mountains in Chile and Argentina. It is a conifer, growing male, pollen-producing cones on separate trees from those growing female cones. The female cones are large, about 15 centimetres wide, but they seldom spread their seeds naturally in Britain. Most monkey puzzle trees in Britain have been planted specially.

The branches grow from the trunk in a series of whorls. The leaves are almost triangular in shape, thick and leathery, and end in very sharp spines. They grow all along the stems and branches, overlapping each other with their spiny tips.

▲ *Monkey puzzle trees have nothing at all to do with monkeys, but they have a strange appearance.*

Monkey puzzles were popular in Victorian gardens for their curiosity value. In South America, the seeds were collected for food.

◄ *The spiky, overlapping leaves of a monkey puzzle tree growing on a shoot from the base of the trunk.*

COMMON CONIFERS IN PLANTATIONS

A plantation of trees is a crop, just like wheat or sugar beet, but unlike these crops, trees are not harvested every year. It may take over forty years before the trees are ready for felling. Conifers are often planted because they grow more quickly than many broadleaved trees, and because the wood of some conifers, such as spruce, pine, grand fir or western hemlock can be pulped and used to make paper. Spruce wood is especially suitable for making paper, because it is pale, with no dark-coloured heartwood. Many people do not like the large, dark plantations of conifers that have been planted and grown over much of the countryside, especially in the west and north of Britain. But the demand for wood and wood pulp is never-ending. Think how much paper you use in a week. All round the world, the paper that each person uses adds up to over 3,000 million tonnes a year!

▲ *Male cones of noble fir are crimson, round and tiny, only 6 millimetres wide. They shed masses of powdery pollen.*

Noble fir

Scientific name: *Abies procera*
Height: up to 47 metres
Bark: silvery or purplish grey, with resin blisters, developing cracks
Introduced

Noble fir and grand fir (*Abies grandis*) are tall fir trees from western North America. Noble fir has dark-green, long narrow needles that are leathery and blunt at the tip. Grand fir has similarly shaped needles, which smell strongly of oranges or tangerines when they are bruised. Noble fir has large, cylindrical cones that grow upright on sturdy shoots near the top of the crown. The female cones break up while still on the tree, shedding their sticky, resinous scales and seeds on to the floor below.

Sitka spruce

Scientific name: *Picea sitchensis*
Height: up to 55 metres
Bark: purplish-grey, cracking into small plates
Introduced

Sitka spruce from western North America is the most important tree of the British forestry industry. A greater area of this spruce is planted than any other conifer, and together with Norway spruce, it accounts for over half of all conifer wood produced in Britain. Sitka spruce has stiff, 2.5-centimetre-long needles, which end in sharp points. The cones are short and sausage-shaped, with each thin, brown scale crinkled along its edge.

▶ *Sitka spruce grows quickly so it can produce a lot of timber, much of which is used by the paper industry.*

Western hemlock

Scientific name: *Tsuga heterophylla*
Height: up to 46 metres
Bark: brown, becoming shredded and flaked
Introduced

Western hemlock leaves can be distinguished from other conifers with flat, narrow needles because they are uneven in size on the same shoot. The needles along the tops of each shoot are half the length of those running in rows below, which measure about 1.7 centimetres in length. At the top of a western hemlock tree, the leading shoot is curved over. The tree has small, hanging cones of just 2.5 centimetres long.

◀ *Western hemlocks have a dense, pyramid-shaped crown.*

Lodgepole pine

Scientific name: *Pinus contorta var. latifolia*
Height: up to 25 metres
Bark: dark-brown, squared plates, with reddish-brown cracks
Introduced

▼ *Lodgepole pines grow well in sandy soils.*

Lodgepole pine is another conifer grown for its wood which, like so many of our commercially important trees, comes from western North America. The bright-green, twisted needles are about 6 centimetres long and grow in pairs. The cones are small, no more than 6 centimetres long, but can be identified by a long thorn at the tip of each scale.

CONIFER	USE OF WOOD
Noble fir	Pallets, kitchen furniture and other joinery.
Grand fir	Pallets, kitchen furniture and other joinery.
Sitka spruce	Plywood, structural timbers, pallets, boxes and crates, wood pulp for paper.
Western hemlock	Plywood, structural timbers, pallets, boxes and crates, wood pulp for paper.

Be a Tree Detective

Learning how to identify different trees and shrubs is a bit like detective work. Every species is different, so you will need to look for clues. Take a notebook and a pencil, and make notes and drawings of the trees close to your home or school. Then look them up in this book, or other books about trees.

To identify a tree, first, look at its overall size and the shape of its crown. Then look at the shape of its leaves. Are they a simple shape with a continuous outline, like a beech leaf, or divided into many leaflets, like an ash leaf? Next look at the bark: is it smooth or rough? Are the flowers large and coloured, or are they small and hanging in catkins? If it is evergreen and the leaves are narrow needles, can you find any cones?

Remember, evergreen trees look almost the same all year round, but deciduous trees look very different in the winter compared to the summer. Many of the trees that you will see in Britain and Europe have flowers that open before the leaves unfurl in the spring. In the summer, the leaves may hide the developing fruits, but in autumn these fruits ripen and the ground below the tree may be carpeted with them. Keep a look out for all these changes, to help you to identify trees and shrubs.

▲ *Rowan leaves are compound – each leaf is divided up into a number of smaller leaflets.*

▼ *These red oak leaves have a simple shape, with lobes that end in points.*

▼ *Catkins are made up of many smaller flowers, which are usually pollinated by the wind. Each male flower produces masses of dry, dusty pollen.*

▼ *Insect-pollinated trees and shrubs, like these gorse shrubs, usually have large, brightly coloured flowers.*

WINTER TWIGS

Even in winter it is possible to distinguish one tree from another. After the leaves have fallen, it is much easier to see the shape of the twigs and how they grow out from the branches. Some, such as silver birch and weeping willow, have slender drooping twigs, others, such as oak and horse chestnut have thicker twigs that point upwards.

Pick some leafless winter twigs and study them closely. You should be able to see the scars left when the leaves fell in the autumn. Next year's buds will be at the sides and tips of each twig. Inside tough bud scales, the tiny young leaves will be tightly folded. The bud scales protect these delicate leaves from damage. Most of these buds are very small, but those of a horse chestnut are large – if you carefully pull off the sticky bud scales, you can see how the new leaf is packed inside. You may even find the tiny flower buds. You may also notice little pale dots on the bark of each twig. These are called lenticels. They are tiny holes through which oxygen from the air enters the twig. Even plants have to breathe!

▼ *Birch twigs (below left) are slender, with small, pointed buds. Horse chestnut twigs (below right) are thick, with fat, sticky buds.*

LEAF RUBBINGS

To make leaf rubbings, you will need:
- leaves collected from trees and shrubs
- a sheet of card or thick paper
- a sheet of thin white paper
- soft coloured pencils or crayons
- sticky tape

1. Lay a leaf flat on the card.
2. Place the white paper on top.
3. Stick down the edges of the paper with sticky tape.
4. Rub gently over the paper and leaf using a coloured pencil or crayon. A perfect outline of the leaf should appear, together with its fine network of veins.
5. At the bottom of each rubbing, write the name of the tree the leaf came from. Keep the rubbings in a special folder, so you can have your own leaf identification guide.

Planting Trees

Growing your own trees from seeds that you have gathered yourself can be fun. You need to start looking for seeds in the autumn, since this is the time when most trees shed their fruits. The easiest seeds to find are those of oak, horse chestnut, ash, sycamore and pine. Collect some acorns, chestnuts (conkers), ash and sycamore 'keys'. If you can find a freshly fallen, unopened pine cone, put it in a warm place until it opens, then shake out the seeds.

PLANTING A TREE

You will need:

- a flowerpot for each type of seed you have collected
- some garden soil
- some labels

1. Collect some acorns, conkers, ash and sycamore 'keys'.

2. Fill each flowerpot with soil and plant the seeds so that they are just covered with earth.

3. Label each pot.

4. Dig small holes in an empty area of flowerbed and stand each pot inside.

The pots can be left outside all winter. Next spring, you should have your very own collection of tree seedlings. If lots of seedlings appear in one pot, separate them out into a pot each. When they get too big for their pots, they will need to be planted out into the ground. Young trees will need watering until they become established. Remember that trees grow very tall, so do not plant them too close to your house.

▲ *When seedlings get too big for their pots, they need planting in the ground.*

◀▼ *You may be surprised how many tree seeds you can find in the autumn, even in a city park. Look out for the seeds shown here, from left to right: chestnuts (conkers), acorns, field maples and pine cones.*

PLANTING TREES IN TOWNS

Trees and shrubs in towns and cities help to keep our air clean by trapping airborne pollutants. They also provide shelter for birds, shade for people in the summer and they make our surroundings more attractive whatever the season.

There are many different kinds of places where trees can be planted in towns. Some, such as parks, playgrounds, reclaimed industrial sites or inner-city development projects are large. Trees that grow large can be planted here, such as ash, beech, birch, horse chestnut or oak. Other urban sites may be much smaller, such as shopping precincts and car parks, the grounds around office blocks, gardens or the centres of roundabouts. Trees that will not grow too tall are best for these sites, such as rowan, some kinds of maple, or ornamental flowering cherries.

THREATS

Trees produce thousands if not millions of seeds in a lifetime, but very few of these sprout and survive to become full-grown. Some seeds are killed by fungi, some compete with too many other seeds, and others do not land in the right place to grow. Young trees may be eaten by deer or rabbits. City streets can be like deserts in the summer, especially for a newly planted, young tree. If a new tree has been planted outside your house in hot, dry weather, you can help it survive by watering it. If young trees live through these early hazards, they can survive for a very long time.

▲ *These saplings are being planted on a housing estate in London.*

TELLING THE AGE OF TREES

You can work out the age of a felled tree by counting the number of rings on its trunk. Every year, as the trunk grows thicker, another ring appears, so each ring equals one year. Next time you see a felled tree, see if you can tell how old it is. The oldest trees in the world are bristlecone pine trees from Arizona. They are thought to be about 5,000 years old. In Britain and Europe, the oldest recorded trees are yews, which can live to over 800 years. Oaks can live for up to 500 years, and sweet chestnuts and others are known to reach 300 years. Birch trees, however, will usually only live for 70–100 years.

▶ *The rings on this damson tree trunk show the amount of growth the tree has made every year. By counting the rings, you can tell the age of the tree.*

Glossary

Arboretum (plural arboreta) A place where many different kinds of trees, often from different parts of the world, are planted for research or recreation.

Aril A fleshy layer that grows up around the seeds of some kinds of plants, for example yew.

Berry A type of fleshy fruit containing a number of seeds.

Botanists People who study plants.

Bract A leaf-like layer that often surrounds a flower head or cone.

Bud scales The protective layers that enclose a leaf bud until it is ready to open in spring.

Burrs Rough lumps that grow on the trunks of trees such as the black poplar.

Catkins A hanging flower head that is made up of many tiny, usually wind-pollinated, flowers.

Compound A leaf that is made up of a number of leaflets.

Cone Parts of a conifer that bear seeds or produce pollen.

Coppicing The practice of cutting the shoots of new trees down at ground level every few years.

Crown The part of a tree made up of its leafy, spreading branches.

Cultivated A tree that is deliberately planted for a particular purpose, such as for its nuts, fruit, decorative leaves or timber.

Cuttings Short lengths of twig which, when cut and planted, sprout roots and grow into a new tree or shrub.

Deciduous A tree that sheds all its leaves in autumn.

Disperse To spread out.

Evergreen A tree or shrub that has leaves all year round.

Germinate When a seed starts to sprout and grow.

Grove A small group of trees.

Heartwood The central part of a tree trunk, which is often deeply coloured and the best part to use for making furniture.

Husk The thin, dry outer covering of some types of fruits.

Hybrid A cross between two different species of trees, shrubs and other living things.

Immune Resistant to infection.

Introduced A tree or shrub that has been planted in a country where it is not found naturally.

Laxative A substance that speeds up the passage of faeces through the bowels.

Leaflets Small leaves.

Lenticels Tiny holes in the bark of trees or shrubs through which gases such as oxygen and carbon dioxide can pass in or out.

Lobe A rounded part.

Marquetry A craft where thin layers of wood are inserted into a wooden surface to produce a decorative effect.

Native A tree or shrub that occurs naturally in a country.

Nutrients Food substances needed in order to live, grow and reproduce.

Plantations Areas where large numbers of trees are planted as a crop to be harvested for their timber.

Pollarding The practice of cutting the branches of a tree's crown back to the top of the trunk.

Pollination The process by which pollen is carried from the male part of a flower or cone to the female part of a flower or cone of the same kind.

Seedlings A very young plant that has just sprouted from a germinating seed.

Shoots The young stems of a tree or shrub.

Silt The sediment of mud and fine sand that is deposited by a river or stream.

Species A particular type of tree, shrub or other living organism that can usually only reproduce with others of the same kind.

Spray A spreading shoot or twig with its leaves or flowers.

Stamens The parts of the flower that contain the pollen, consisting of a slender stem, called the filament, with an anther at the tip.

Suckers Twiggy shoots that grow up from the roots around the base of a tree.

Thicket A tangled mass of shrubs or young trees.

Timber Wood for building or carpentry.

Var. An abbreviation for 'variety'.

Veins Fine ribs in a leaf which carry water and dissolved nutrients.

Veneer A thin layer of wood or other material.

Whorl A ring of leaves, flowers or branches growing around a stem.

Further Information

BOOKS TO READ

Cycles in Nature: Plant Life by Theresa Greenaway (Hodder Wayland, 2000)

Eyewitness Handbook: Trees by Allen J. Coombes (Dorling Kindersley, 1994)

Life in a Giant Tree in the Rainforest by Sally Morgan (Belitha, 1999)

Looking at Animals in Trees by Moira Butterfield (Belitha, 1999)

Nature and Science: Leaves by Taylor Burton (Watts, 1997)

Plants: British Trees, British Plants, How Plants Grow by Angela Royston (Heinemann, 1999)

Straightforward Science: Plant Life by Peter Riley (Watts, 1998)

The Earth Strikes Back: Plant Life by Pamela Grant (Belitha, 1999)

WEBSITES

Forestry Commission: www.forestry.gov.uk

Friends of the Earth: www.foe.co.uk

National Trust: www.nationaltrust.org.uk

Royal Botanical Gardens, Kew: www.rbgkew.org.uk

The Natural History Museum: www.nhm.ac.uk

PLACES TO VISIT

Places where many different kinds of trees are grown are called arboreta. Trees in arboreta are usually labelled, which helps you to get to know them. Here are a few places to visit:

Birr Castle, Co. Offaly, Eire

Bodnant, Tal y Cefn, Conway

Castlewellan, Newcastle, Co. Down, N. Ireland

National Pinetum, Bedgebury, Kent

Royal Botanic Gardens, Edinburgh

Royal Botanic Gardens, Kew, London

Syon House, Brentford

Wakehurst Place, Sussex

Westonbirt Arboretum, Gloucestershire

Windsor Great Park, Berkshire

Winkworth Arboretum, Surrey

Index

Page numbers in **bold** refer to photographs.

48